FROM BAR STOOLS TO CHURCH PEWS

Volume One

To My Soldier girl

I Love ya.

Always

D Mckee

x

From Bar Stools To Church Pews

Volume One

Writings by

D. "Red" McKeever

RED TALES
2005

From Bar Stools
To Church Pews
By D. 'Red' McKeever
Copyright 2003
By D. McKeever

Light Skinned
Just Once
The Whole
And I Love Her
Exposed
By D. 'Red' McKeever
Copyright 1984
By D. McKeever

Lift Me Up
Praise Him
Untitled
By D. 'Red' McKeever
Copyright 2005
By D. McKeever

Published by Red Tales

ISBN 0–9760149–0-4

PRINTED IN THE UNITED STATES OF AMERICA
BY
ATHENS PRINTING COMPANY
337 West 36th Street
New York, NY 10018-6401

Contents

Acknowledgement 9

Gone 11
Light Skinned 12
Exposed 13
Heart Holding 14
Gut Reaction 15
Just Once 16
The Whole 17
Sonnet #4 18
And I Love Her 19
Sonnet #2 20
Never Enough 21
I 22
Emptiness 23
Emptiness 2 24
Uprooted 25
Catch Love 26
Wanting and Waiting 27
Life Now 28
Rare Love 29
Deeper Friendship 30
No Rush 31
Me 33
Dreams 34

Sonnet #3 35
Verse Writing 36
Protection 37
Elsewhere 38
Remind Me 39
Hard Places 40
Missing You 41
How Long 42
My Prayer 43
Give and Take 45
I Will Learn 47
Fear 48
Love 49
Once Again 50
Home 51
And This is For You 52
Motion 53
My Lord 54
No Questions 56
Now 58
God Is/Affirmation 60
Available 61
Ask 62
Call Him 63
This Flesh is Just a Shell 64
Come To Me 66
Bless Me Prayer 67
It Is Done 68
Endless Possibilities 69

Passion 70

A Measure 71

When I Look Around 72

Dear Lord Thank You 74

God's Gift 76

On This Day 77

Spirit Told Me 79

Deal With What You Must 80

I Affirm 82

Order My Steps 83

Praises 84

P.U.S.H.—Pray Until Something Happens 85

Blessings 87

I Thank You for All That... 88

Praying My Strength 90

I Will 91

Take Flight 92

It Was Told to Me 93

Mine 95

God's Work 96

Untitled 97

Praise Him 98

Lift Me Up 100

Sonnet #1 102

The Journey Back 103

About the Author 105

Acknowledgements

First and foremost I would like to thank God for calling out my name in a voice that I can recognize.

Thank you Wade and Dorothy, my parents, who gave me love the only way that they knew how to give it.

To my siblings and their spouses, if it weren't for your unconditional love I would have been squashed like a bug. Thank you.

To my natural family here and beyond, thank you for all of your support and encouragement.

To my church family and friends, thank you for allowing me to share.

To Lynn, thank you for letting me share my past and thank you for wanting to share my future. I love you.

Lastly, thank you God (yet again) for seeing this ending from the beginning. Thank you for all that You have given . . . and then some.

—Red

Gone

I often wonder what would you do if anything happened
—to me
—to us.

What changes would you go through.

Or would it be . . . . . .

Another one bites the dust.

Light Skinned

Too many think that being a light skinned
woman is always an easy way.

With no struggle . . .

And doors don't ever slam in my face.

Yet you shut me out everyday, my lonely lover.

Always looking upon me with suspicion and distrust.
Coming to me guarded . . .
As if I were part of the problem.

Letting a stranger's incomplete synopsis of you
Bring you down
And blur your vision.

Always coming in between you and I.

Letting personal preferences and/or envious hearts
sputter words in demeaning ways.

. . . Continuing the absurd folklore of the darker skin.

. . . I carry no such tales.

Exposed

I walked into this situation
with my eyes open.

I was aware of the circumstances in which we were
placed by our undying love—

But I believed in you.

You said that you could love me
like no other.

You said you'd be my clown
and chase my blues away.

You said you'd never hurt me.
So I believed in you.

I trusted you.

I exposed a special part of my being,
one which is not often seen
. . . And you betrayed me.

My emotions were but a toy to be played with—
'til you grew weary of the game.

Heart Holding

Don't want to take anyone
on a trip . . .

So just hold on to your heart

. . . And walk away.

Gut Reactions

Before all the understanding settled in . . .
I wanted to slap your face.
Before I realized that it was partly my fault . . .
I wanted to send you packing . . .
Or better yet . . . wanted to turn and walk out . . .
on cue.
. . . wanted to curse/scream
kick myself in the ass . . .
feeling like such a fool.
Remaining with you still, . . . after . . .
Affairs are easy for you it seems.
A mirrored image of a younger self.
Conveniently, for whatever reason, there will always be
a friend waiting.
Flashing lights of red and yellow flood my mind,
my heart.
Warning me of the possible heartbreak.
Can I live like this- for you play the game all too well . . .
Better than I ever did.
And that thought will always stay in my brain . . .
As I carefully make my way.

Just Once

Just once I would like for you
to ask me to stay.

. . . To plead like I have for you.

Just once I would like to hear you
tell me
how happy and proud you are
of this relationship;

Without having to be prompted.

The Whole

Today's events have shown me that I have,
somewhere along the line
been reduced to just a pussy.

A hole for your tongue to suck out the juices.
A space for your fingers to explore.

Aside from that . . . there could very well . . .
Be nothing.

And when you can't have it your way
for whatever reason . . . there is no way at all.

Misery loves company.

Well I'm here to tell ya
that I don't take kindly to either—
Reduction or misery.

There is more joy in me than what lies
between my legs.

That's just an added attraction.

. . . A part of the whole.

Sonnet #4

Let my touch heat yours
. . . And let our minds unite
As our souls melt into oneness.

And I Love Her

. . . .And I love her.

But she is still going thru a
metamorphosis,
trying to know
herself
me and the world around her.

She is struggling, striving
stretching hard.

And in her struggle
she is hurting
(being a Black creative Gay Female, she's gonna hurt)

She is suspicious.

Trying to know
me
the world around her
and herself.

Hurting inside.

Hurting me outside.

. . . And as I play Face It Girl, It's Over
the reality hits me.

Tears stream down my face, and
. . . I still love her.

Sonnet #2

Just an ordinary woman,
With no fantastic feats to my name.
Making my mistakes as I try to find my way.

Carrying the burden of uncertainty
And not always being able to fit into the spaces provided.

Having the past play hide and seek with the future
Causing an uneven flow.

Joy and pain . . .
Two sides of the same coin.

Never Enough

. . . The release was good
and very much needed,
but it is only temporary.
And just as I received your call
a storm was again rising.
And it will continue to rise . . .
Until my flesh meets yours . . .
Until our bodies have pounded together . . .
Until our bodies ache
And we collapse with exhaustion into each other.

I

Today I started thinking in singular pronouns.
It seems like the only thing left to do.
Because no matter how far we reach out,
we still fall short
. . . too many times.
And sometimes I can't really tell if
that extended hand
is trying to pull me closer . . .
. . . or is it really pushing me away.

Emptiness

Sometimes I think you're living a lie.
Here with me . . . speaking words of love.

Is it all rehearsed? . . . Just something to say
. . . something to make the situation a little more bearable,
for a while anyway.

And this time when you spoke,
the words did not fall down into the depths
of my well.
Did not stir in the darkness of my soul.
They just rippled and skidded on the surface.

. . . And I open my legs—as routine.
Because I know your need.

. . . Is that all it is for you now
—need.
A desire to get off.

. . . Sometimes . . .
I live in the space that is created when love
goes on vacation.

Emptiness 2

What I am offering . . .
you are not able to receive.
And what you think you see . .
is the effects of visual illusions.

And what a pity—for this could have been
a best seller.

It doesn't matter anymore—
I've given up the fight.

For after relating to me—living with me
you still miss the point of my love . . .
stabbing me deep with your doubt.
Leaving my soul to poor out into emptiness.

Uprooted

I was once a beautiful flower
growing lovely, in the warmth of the radiant sun.
A beautiful flower . . . once upon a time,
with stem and pedals of deep rich color.
. . . with roots that ran deep into
the nourishing black soil.

A beautiful flower
until I was walked on . . .
Cut
and plucked.

Taken out of my natural surroundings
. . . my strength
to decorate another corner of your mind.

Transplanted only to die.

Catch Love

Love—
Sometimes even as I hold on tightly,
it still slips through my hands
like sand . . . or water
which I may cup and hold for only a short while.

That no matter how far I stretch,
it is still beyond my reach
beyond my grasp.

No matter how fast I run,
love is always faster.
A few paces ahead
And deep as I may dig into my soul,
love always wants to go deeper
breaking open new spaces.

The closer I look, the more I see that
there is to see.

And just when I'm ready to give up . . .
never again to chase the illusive
. . . it's face comes shining out from behind
the stormy clouds
waiting to start all over again.

Wanting and Waiting

It's always so hard waiting for you
. . . never knowing when it's all right to call.
Waiting on pins and needles.

Missing you.

Lately you never seem to be
far from my thoughts.
I dream about you . . .
both day and night.
Wanting to be with you
. . . everywhere . . .
so that I won't miss that smile or twinkle
in your eyes.
—That sexy far away stare drives me wild.

—Thinking 'bout me?

I see you in my head
and feel you in my soul.

Just maybe it will work
. . . this time 'round.

Life Now

There have been others
. . . before you
but it is only now that my life has taken hold.
It is with you that it is all happening.
. . . maybe because of you.
I just want to say
thank you . . .
for being here with me . . .
for me.

Thank you.

Rare Love

I want to give you a love so rare
so beautiful
that it will surely leave a deep impression upon on soul.
I want to give something special.
Something none other has given—
Perhaps a pearl from Yemeya Olocun.
Or a lovely desert flower for your hair.
A love you will not want to be without.
A love that keeps you coming back.
But what I want to give you most of all is
a real love.
. . . A warm and soft kind of love.
A love that will try to understand
no matter how confused it all seems.
I am here for you, my love
my life.
Me and my poems—
Singing sweetly for your tender ears to hear.
Singing sweetly only for you and your love.

Deeper Friendship

I have always enjoyed my hours of solitude.
My space . . . my time
to reflex . . . daydream
or just do nothing at all.
But now I find that lately, you take up much of this time.
Your unseen image.
I replay our conversations while trying to foresee what
future ones will hold.
I am becoming passionately intense about our friendship.
Feeling a bond forming . . . And desiring more.
To put it simply
I want to be your lover.
Although there is nothing simple about this situation . . .

. . .

. . .

. . . I want to be your lover.

No Rush

Like the gentle snow
that blankets the land during the night . . .
That's how I want to be
. . . so soft.
Like the dew that wets your toes
in the morn
. . . so sweet.

Everyday there is a rush.

But I don't want to rush through this love.

Like the eagle in full flight
and gliding with wings full abreast.
I want to quicken your breath
and make you shiver.

As the lamb romps in the
Pastures of your mind,
I (too) want to play.

And I don't want to rush this love.

I want to feel it coming on me.
Moving around . . .
From my toes . . . to my head.
To my ears . . . and between my thighs.

I want to simmer a bit.
Letting the good smells thicken in the air.

. . . Don't wanna rush . . . no rush.

Just want to hold on for as long as I can
—savoring every minute—
until I can't hold it anymore.

Me

What I am . . .
is a woman.
Wanting you with a woman's passion.

I'm sure about myself..
of who I am.

And I compliment you very well.

Call yourself whatever you want-
I've been there,
And I don't want any more
(of those bad habits.)

I got something new—
Something that works better—
Someone better . . . for me.

And I'm not going to let go.

Dreams

You make my life every bit of what I dreamt it would be
as if you were there so many dreams ago.
. . . And I trust in you to take it (the dream)
further . . .

Sonnet #3

All I want is to care for you
        And help you get to where you have to go.
My presence will not hinder your growth;
            Only enhance it,
                Intensify it.
I will give you new light—
        The me of what I am,
And together we will shine.

Verse Writing

Verse writing in my head about the love I feel
for you.
Sometimes pictures come to my mind and I get lost . . .
Seeing, feeling everything to completion.
And even though it's just a picture in my mind
. . . you take my breath away.
My senses come alive.
My spirit walks with your spirit.
A volcano begins to erupt,
my soul is burning.
Alive with the sense of you all around me.
You . . . weaving in and out of my thoughts/ my heart.
And I . . . wanting no other . . . save you.

Protection

I have tried not to dwell on what has transpired
. . . (Or not transpired) between us in the last few days,
But it is hard.
To think you felt that you had to protect yourself from me.
. . . That I would take away what is not mine.
I thought you knew . . .
I would give you all without thought or reason.
—But you did what you thought you had to do.
And in the mist of it all—
You drifted away.
When did last our lips meet?
Three days? More . . .

You need space, not embraces or hugs.
No T. L. C.
You have too many real situations on your mind.
Dollars and cents.
—Of which I have little of.
—Not emotion.
—Of which I am full of.

Not wanting to smother you
or have my feelings bruised, I step away.

Hopefully soon you will realize that you and I want the same
thing.
We just (might) go about it differently.

Elsewhere

And we both deserve
peace love and happiness

It's unfortunate
that I believe that mine
is with you

. . . And (you think that) yours is elsewhere.

Remind Me

To hear that you have anything other than dislike and mistrust
for the person that helped put me through . . .
Grieves my soul.
The wound is still there.

To hear you say that you feel her pain . . .
Concerns me.

I don't believe that the pain she expresses cuts deep.

I think that she uses whatever she can . . .
To control whomever she can.
And right now . . . it's you.

And when, unknowingly,
I begin to melt into your being . . . (once again)
I am reminded
That this battle is mine
And I am standing alone.

Hard Places

I hope you are never in this place
where all things, as they are now..
are magnified in your face.
Where your present quickly becomes your past . . .
at no choice of your own.

A place where no matter how good
it looks . . .
you still question the very core of your being.

And still the answers are vague . . . if at all.

This is a hard place to be.
Day in and day out.
And even a harder place to live.

. . . But I am here living in it everyday.

Missing You

Someone is always trying to intellectualize this
. . . even me.
When sometimes it just comes down to . . .

I'm going to miss your touch
Your smell
And the warmth of your body.
Your breath
Your softness.

I'm going to miss your kisses
And the juices that lies between your thighs
. . . even though never a taste have I tasted.
You've been good to me.
Thank you.

And I will miss your expressive eyes
Your tender lips.
And that fantastic beautiful exotic face.

I will miss . . .
Spending the rest of my life with you.

How Long

How long have I waited to have my dream
                         . . . my vision
come before mine eyes.

I have seen you—all too many times
                         . . . In my head.
                         . . . In my heart.
Standing just as you do now.

I have needed you-
All of my life.
Looking and searching
                         . . . Trying so many things.
Where have you been?
And why has it taken you so long to come to me.
Peace in my soul
                         In my home.
How long I have waited.
Longing in the pits of my heart.
Grasping on to all the ghosts.
And clinging still . . . long after the visionary image had
    disappeared.

But you are not a visionary image.
You are every bit—real.

And I will want and need you always.

My Prayer

Because I made her my world
it is very difficult for me to put a "H" on my back
and handle it (the break up).

Because I thought that our love would last
a life time,
the realization that it has not
makes me cry and move forward timidly.

Acceptance is hard.
I still cling to a past that has pushed beyond
my gasp.
Clinging for dear life
Or near death . . .
I don't know anymore.

My Prayer
God please give me the strength to endure
whatever situation you have allowed to transpire
in my life.
Let your will be done.
Give me the strength to accept your will.

I need your help and your peace.
You know better than I what I am in need of.
I look to you to provide (for) my needs.
I walk out on faith upon today
for I can not see the end from where I
currently stand.
Only you can.

I ask that you give me courage to move forward
into unknown territories.
Keep me safe, away from harm.
Guide and direct me.
Counsel me with your infinite wisdom.

Open the windows
where the doors has been shut.
Bless me.
Bless me.
Bless me, my merciful Father.

I ask that you bind the spirit of jealously and resentment.
The spirit of injury and suicide.

I ask that you singe all ties that keep
me bound to this place.

I ask for your forgiveness.

Give and Take

If I take on all the responsibility,
what happens to the self worth
of my partner?

If I make all of the decisions,
what happens to the valve of her
decision making devices?

If I never tell her of the problem,
never ask help in finding a solution,
what happens to her ability to handle such and to
grow from . . . ?
How will you ever learn to walk
if I always carry you.

A relationship is giving and taking.
Not taking and then
taking some more.
Giving and taking.
An exchange;
Affording each to bring to the table
all of their knowledge and experiences.

How can I take that from you . . .
Why would I want to.

Your experiences are just as important and valuable.
Your knowledge just as vast.
You and I are on equal ground.

Giving and taking.
Taking and giving.
This is a relationship.
Not one, but both being responsible.
Holding back nothing.
Growing.
. . . And sometimes growth is painful.
But in the end
it will be better for both.

I Will Learn

I will learn to trust myself.
To pat myself on the back.
To look in the mirror and say,
"Hi Pretty Lady" or "Good Job".
To live uninvolved with anyone other than those
that can add to my awareness; and I to theirs.

I will learn to put aside all BS from BS people.
Not concerning myself with hurting their ego
by saying what has to be said.
And to go along with NOTHING that is contrary
to me and my beliefs.

I must learn that I AM just as IMPORTANT.

Fear

I am afraid to put down on paper
all that it was,
and all that it was not.

Is it because that once it is written, I will
have to face up to the facts that it wasn't working
. . . and hasn't for a while.
Would have to realize how I compromised
and settled for something less . . . just
to be/stay together.
Trying to force the fit.

I . . . settling for whatever I could get
just to be with you.

Sometimes I felt short changed.
But I didn't want/was afraid to leave.

Was afraid to see you with another.
I thought I could be your world.

In my own way, I thought that I was protecting you
from an unknown world.
. . . But I was being fearful and protective.
Adding to the stress I was trying to relieve.

I'm sorry, my diamond.

I wanted everyone to see . . .
But only from afar.

Love

All I can do now . . .
Is say that I love you with all of my heart and soul
. . . and hope that you feel it
And know it is truth.

Once Again

It almost happened again.
Almost made you my world
Seeing no other
Not even my GOD.

But then you asked me to sign
On the dotted line.
Assuring that your investment would always
Be remembered.

I signed.
And found reality once more.

Home

. . . And still another setback.

Seems like not too many things have gone right
since I've been "on my own."

Feeling so misplaced.
Life and changes,
setbacks and recoveries.

But now my body grows weary
and I'm not so quick to snap back.

. . . sometimes I get too tired to even care.

Thinking back—
if I had to do it over . . .
there would be some changes made.

Home.
I wanna go home . . .
. . . wherever that (home) is.

And This is For You . . .

It's been quite some time since I have had a tranquil thought
leading to a source of inspiration to write.
And the thought is you.
You have been on my mind this entire weekend.
Wanting to hold you close to me
. . . without interruption
. . . without reservation.
Wanting to look into your eyes
. . . onto your face
. . . your body.
At times, just the thought of you
takes my breath away (. . . rush).
You have imprinted my soul.
Somehow-somewhere,
with your being and no matter how much I try
to kid myself
. . . I know that this is true.
My body is starting to crave yours.
I sit . . . and close my eyes
And try to remember when last we touched.
I miss you.

Motion

What makes you think that you can wait until you move
before you get set into motion.
You can't.
Start accelerating now in order not to be left in the starting
blocks.

You have the ability.
You have the knowledge.
You have God.

Thank you Jesus.

Just do it!

My Lord

My Lord
I've been waiting
I've been waiting.
My Lord.

My Lord
I've been crying
I've been crying.
My Lord.

My Lord
I've been searching
I've been searching.
My Lord.

My Lord
I've been kneeling
I've been kneeling.
My Lord.

My Lord
I've been praying
I've been praying
My Lord.

My Lord
I've been healing
I've been healing.
My Lord.

My Lord
I've been kneeling
I've been praying.
My Lord.

My Lord
I've been healing
I've been healing.
My Lord.

No Questions

Not wanting to offend
Always wanting to fit in
Things are said . . .
Hurtful hateful words
(just overlook them)

Not wanting to offend
Only wanting to fit in
Hands touch
Fingers prey and pinch
. . . Sometimes it's good
but most of the time
. . . not.
Wanting not to offend
Always wanting to fit in
(you) remain silent
wishing for quick resolution.
So you can go on with your life.

Not wanting to offend
Just wanting to fit in.

Can't tell anyone.
Everyone is part of the game.
(And the game is you.)
Brothers, sister, cousins
and friends galore.

Always trying to fit in
Wanting not to offend.
(your) voice is taken away.
There is no power.

Just push it away.
Bury it and live on.

There is no power.
No power.

No. No More.

No power . . . until now.

Now

Writing reflexes the extremes of my life.

I write either when I am very high
. . . or very low.
There is no middle ground.

Knowing this I began to evaluate my
prayer life.
And I've come to realize that it is the same.

I pray when I am delighted and full of joy.
. . . Pray even more when I am disillusioned or hurt.

And the middle ground is the everyday
hustle and bustle
. . . 9 to 5.
Clocking in and clocking out.

But shouldn't we be thankful for that also.

Of course we should.

So how can I show my middle ground as a reflection of my
gratitude
and appreciation . . . for the NOW (wherever NOW is).
Giving it the time and space
the importance that it deserves.
For all of us only have NOW.

And NOW is when GOD wants to hear our praises.

Now is when we need to lift HIM up.
Now is when we need to share HIS love and HIS words
with others.
NOW is all we have.

Can't wait until that promotion comes through.
Or when the test comes back . . . negative.
We can't wait until tomorrow, for
that is not promised.

What is promised is everlasting life for them
that seek HIS face
that know HIM
love HIM
. . . and believe in HIM.

But you must thank HIM now.
Love HIM and believe in HIM
NOW.

Plant HIS words as seeds in your soul
NOW.

For NOW is all we have.

God Is / Affirmation

I affirm that God is my everything
from which all things flow.

With Her we are everything.

Without Her we are nothing.

Available

No matter what my circumstances are . . .

She is always available.

All I have to do is call her name . . .

Any time

Any where.

Ask

In order to hear from the Lord
You must be active in the process
. . . And so it is written
"Ask and you shall receive" . . .

But first, you must ask.
And no two answers are the same.
Yours might allow you to jump and shout
—speak in tongue—.
Yet mine, might allow me to sit at peace
quiet and serene.

Neither experience displays a more powerful anointing
—more love or more devotion.

Each Does display the power of the Almighty in
YOU . . .
And in ME.

But first we must ask.

Call Him

Lord, God, my Savior

AB, Father, Mother

Jehovah, Allah, Elohim

El Sadday, my Redeemer.

His name is glorious.

Just speaking His name changes situations;

for His name is wonderful.

This Flesh Is Just A Shell

I thank you ABBA (father)
For all.
. . . All that you have ever given to me.

I thank you for including me in your unique plan.
For stretching out your arms engulfing me and pulling me out
of every situation that I put myself in.
. . . For shining light onto my darkest points.

I thank you for your LOVE.

I thank you for each d

              r

                o

                  p of your BLOOD.

The BLOOD that washes me clean.

I have an abundance of all that I need and could ever want.
For YOU are a great provider.

. . . And it's not that I'm not grateful . . . because I am.

But I find myself coming to YOU again . . . with my needs.

What I am seeking now is your strength and courage . . . to
continue to have faith and believe
that YOU are an all-knowing and ever present GOD.

LORD of lords. KING of kings.

That YOU are still in control . . . even in times of trouble and
   unrest.

I know this in my heart.
But my humanness shows up . . . and fear sets in.

What if . . .
How safe will I be . . . ?
And what about Lynn and the kids, my mom, her mom . . .

Dear LORD, save me from myself.

What can I do alone . . . Nothing.

I need YOU more now then ever.

I have so much to loose and yet without you
   . . . I have already lost.

Spirit of the Lord fall fresh upon me.
Anoint me again and again.
Light my way.
Pull me up and keep me safe wrapped in your loving arms.
Give me strength and courage in my time of need.
Allow me to keep my eye on the prize . . .
   . . . Of life everafter.

Have me to remember that
   . . . this flesh is but a shell.
And to be absent in the flesh is to be with the LORD.

Come To ME

. . . And HE said: Come to ME and I will give you rest.

I need rest upon today Dear Lord.
I need to find peace and comfort.
I am weary.
But still the battle rages on . . .

Renew my spirit oh Lord.
Rain down YOUR strength that will allow me just to stand.

Strength enough to look out of the way . . .
And let YOU handle it.

Bless Me Prayer

Highest Praises to my Creator.

I turn my life over to You.

Let Your will be done.

Place my feet on a crowded path
That I may continually be a witness to all
Your blessings, Your goodness and grace

. . . As I make my way to the prize.

It Is Done

The answers have already been spoken.
You already know why . . .

What you pray for now is acceptance and strength
to let My will be done in your life.
Pray for continued counsel,
acceptance and strength.

Faith will get you through.
Trust in Me.

Concentrate on me.
As I on you.
No one knows better than I,
what you are going through.
It's okay.

I will deliver you
And we will be on the other side, together.

Hang on.
It is well worth the pain and suffering.

I am here with you.
I am waiting for you.

. . . But it is for you to decide.

Endless Possibilities

Endless possibilities . . . is the thought of the day.

I am already well beyond where others said I would/ could be.

Endless possibilities . . .

Doors keep opening.

Opportunities keep presenting themselves (to me).

I see them now . . .

And have the courage to seize the day.

Endless possibilities . . .

Taking that dream and making it real.

Changing that situation around so that

it is working for my good.

God bless the child that takes the steps toward

the endless possibilities that He has promised.

. . . And we are all children sitting at the Master's feet.

Endless possibilities are within your reach . . .

Stretch for yours right now.

Passion

If it is your passion . . .
It will sustain you.

I am passionate about God.
For He gives me the ability to do all
that I love to do.
Therefore He has to be on a higher plane
then that
that I do love.

I am passionate about God.
Praising his name has become an everyday event.
I am passionate about God.
For He is my compass and my light.

I am thankful
that I am passionate about God.

A Measure

A true measure of the God in you
is when you live and practice Her teachings
. . . daily.

Remember to reach out with loving kindness
to family and strangers alike.

When I Look Around

When I look around to see all that I am and all that I have
I need to say Thank You to my God.

I can remember when I was young,
dreaming of how and where I wanted to be at certain stages of
life.

I can remember so many people saying no.
No you couldn't. No you wouldn't.
Just because of who you are . . .
Of what you are.

Well, I'm here to put all doubt to rest.

God knows me and She loves me anyway.

She has continues to open doors that were not only closed, but
locked.
Tight.
She continues to plant my feet on blessed ground.
She continues to provide for me beyond my far- reaching
dreams.
And she continues to give me the desires of my heart.

She loves me anyhow.

She has blessed every effort that I have made in Jesus' name.
She protects me from my enemies.
She even protects me from myself.

God is still in the blessing business.
And She continues to bless me.
Knowing who I am . . .
And yes . . .
Knowing what I am.

Dear Lord Thank You

Lord, I thank You.
And I praise your name.
I praise your name, Glorious Father.
I thank You today, dear Lord for all your wonderful gifts.
I thank You for your tender mercies and your grace.
I thank You for giving me another day.
I thank You for your salvation and your peace.

But what I thank You for most, upon today
Is your acceptance of me.
Knowing me for who I am . . . and loving me
Anyway.

Though You know where I have been . . . And where
I will end up
You still love me, my heavenly Father.

I thank You Lord Jesus for never forsaking me.
For being the first one there . . .
Never to leave.

Oh, I thank You for your presence in my life.

I thank You for not throwing me back
For my lack of . . .
I thank you for not throwing me back
For my inability to . . .
Not throwing me back
Because I am sometimes lost and in need.

With you, dear Lord, I don't have to put it on
Or take it off, to make it fit.
To make it work.

You are just where I am
And I thank You for accepting me at this place.

You are my true friend.
And I thank You.

God's Gift

My walk with God gives me . . .

Infinite possibilities, boundlessness, abundance, joy, understanding,

A guided journey, appreciation for life and all living things,

Strength, courage, meaning, love, self-love, compassion,

Companionship, protection, and motivation.

What does she give to you?

Stop and think for just a moment and create your own list of blessings.

You will soon realize, as I, that your list will not end at the end of the page . . .

and you will have to continue each day to add on another blessing.

My walk with God opens doors and sheds light to the darkest corner.

My walk has transformed me.

I know it has done the same for you.

My walk is . . . Your walk is . . . life . . .

A gift given by the Almighty.

So receive . . . and say thank you in song

and praise

and prayer.

Gift giver, I thank you.

On This Day

On this day I have the privilege to state that I have it all.
God has blessed me, tremendously.
With gifts greater than I could ask for or even imagine.

One such gift is the recognition that he didn't have to do it.
He didn't have to forgive me.
He didn't have to love me.
He didn't have to fill my cup so full that it runs over and over
with mercy and joy.

But he did.

And I love him for it.

Another such gift is the knowledge that his love for me and
mine for the world . . . flows together, seamlessly.
My life, as it is, is not contrary to the Word.
For if it were . . . why would there be Lynn.

Our relationship is so blessed, you don't even know half the
story.
She is truly a gift from God to me.

She has been there to help me through the rough times, when I
was growing
into me.
She has guided me through my indecisions
sharing her family and her love.

And she has been faithful and held on to her belief . . . In God
first . . . and then . . . in me.

There is nothing I can do or say to express my gratitude or my
love.

I will forever be in God's debt.
He saw what I needed and provided.

I am a living witness.

Look at me and see God's love at work.

Spirit Told Me

Spirit told me not to hold back on spreading the Good News.

Not to hesitate to say "God Bless You",

. . . And tell of the Love that He has for ALL of us.

Don't be selective or afraid.

If I truly believe in His blessings and He has blessed me . . .

It is my responsibility to pass the blessing on.

Those that are meant to receive the message . . . will.

Who knows . . . ?

A door just might open or a light might shine for someone that has lost his or her way.

Spirit told me

That if I truly love Him . . . let my love shine.

Drench those around me with the same love as He has for me.

Someone needs to hear His love.

Someone needs to feel His love.

Someone needs to see His love.

And I might be the vessel of choice this time . . . for someone.

Spirit told me

Don't hesitate and don't be afraid.

I am the vessel for someone.

Deal With What You Must

God created us . . .
Blew life into our lifeless bodies for us to become.
She allows situation to transpire,
To give us lessons to place into the book of life.
. . . That we may go back and review whenever necessary.
But deal with what you must and abandon the rest.

She allows friendships to form in order for us to share
What she has imparted to us.

She allows joy and love to come, to fill our lonely nights
And allow our hearts to take flight . . .
As if we were birds up high
Soaring to the unknown.
Deal with what you must and abandon the rest.

She allows life and death to enter
To keep us focus on what is really real,
Giving us time and time again to go back to the drawing board
And plan what goes on . . . in between.
Deal with what you must- abandon the rest.

(my) God is a loving and merciful God.
Giving us free will.
However, the blueprint has already been sketched.
The script already written.

And if we follow the prompts and cues we're given, our lives
will be filled
with love, peace and happiness.
When we learn to turn it all over to God
. . . allow her to be your keeper.
. . . learn to trust and obey
We will be spiritually instructed.
And then we can truly begin to learn
HOW TO DEAL WITH WHAT WE MUST AND ABANDON
THE REST.

I Affirm

I affirm, Lord God, that you are the creator of all.
I honor You.
I praise You.
I worship You.

Order My Steps

I turn my life over to you,
dear Lord.
I await your voice
to give me direction.

Praises

It wasn't any particular word that made me want to jump
And shout.
. . . But rather a constant song filling me up on the inside.

I was having church with myself.
Giving Her praise.
Giving Her prayer.
Giving Her thanks.

Giving Her thanks, praise and prayer
For all the many things She has given to me.
Both large and small.
Past, present and future.

P.U.S.H.
Pray Until Something Happens

It is easy to trust Him when everything is alright
—going smoothly and according to your plan.
But the real trust comes when the plans go astray,
and you don't understand . . . why.
Such is the case at this juncture of my life.

Leaving all the particulars for you to fill in to
accommodate your own (life) story.

Realize first
As you pray everyday
. . . I return myself back to You.
. . . I give my lover and this relationship back to you . . .
That these are not mere words to Him.
-That these words invite Him in.
And He will come.

Be mindful of what you pray for.
He will come and He will deliver you out of.

And when he does deliver you
Praise Him.
Through all of your questions and doubt
Praise Him.

Continue to push your flesh down in order that His spirit will
rise up
Again . . . and again . . . and again.

Sing and shout for joy.
Release yourself of the burden
And let His will be done.

For we are His plan.
He will deliver.
And in the end . . . it will all be good.

Blessings

HE loves us and believes in us.
HE wants us to do better and to reach higher.
HE knows that we can.
He knows that we will.
HE is our guide.
HE is our only true source of strength and knowledge.

Know HIM
And you will know blessings.
Love HIM
And you will know joy.
Keep HIS spirit
And you will know peace
Overflowing and abundantly.

PRAISE the name of our LORD.

I Thank You for All That . . .

I will praise you dear Lord for waking me up this morning.
I will praise you for my strength and health.
I will praise you for the mountains and the wind.

And I will praise you for all that there is.
All that I miss thanking you for as I praise your name.

I know that without you, I am nothing.
I would be wandering around, aimlessly.
I would be lost.

So I praise you for giving me direction.
For planting my feet on solid ground . . . for your guidance.

I praise your name, Abba Father for your faithfulness.
For your loving kindness and your wisdom.

And I will praise you for all that there is.
All that I might miss as I say my prayers morning, noon and at
night.

You see the more I praise your name, the more you reveal
yourself to me . . .
And the more I see that there is to praise your name.

So Heavenly Father,

My Provider.

My Healer.

My Sword and my Shield.

Sometimes all I can say is . . .
Thank you for all that . . . and then some.

May your blessings continue to fall down on me as I praise
your name.

Praying for My Strength

God is my deliverer and my provider.
He has set me up on a rock –high.
He has cut all of the emotional strings that tie me to you,
He has told me "you are delivered from the pain" . . .
I heard Him and I thanked Him.
I felt the release.

. . . Yet it's my flesh that pulls me back into the thick of things.
Back into an unsafe place.
Back into all the hurt and pain.
And it is my flesh that keeps me there.

Prayer:

God, I pray that You strengthen me to push
my fleshly desires down
under my feet,
That I may walk on it everyday.
Allowing only Your spirit to guide and keep me.

I Will

I will never tire.
I will never give up on you.
I will always keep you safe.
I will always make a way.

JUST CALL ME.

I will always answer.
I am here waiting
Wanting to help.
wanting to heal and comfort.

Never doubt MY Love for you;
for I will love always.

Take Flight

Thank you for opening up my soul
allowing me to experience so many beautiful and
deep thoughts/feelings.

Thank you for giving me the time
to see that all my possibilities are . . .
indefinite.

Thank you for giving me the strength
and courage to fight the battles
and the faith to win.

It Was Told to Me

I brought you this far
Not will I leave you.
Trust Me.
Have faith in Me.
This is the beginning.
Say yes.
Say yes.

Lift yourself up.
Feel My presence.
Feel My strength.
Feel My peace.
Not will I leave you.

Lift yourself up.
Feel My love.
Feel My comfort.
Hear My counsel.
Let Me direct your way.

Say yes.
Say yes.

Keep this convenient
And I will provide all things to you.

Never leave from this place . . . here with Me.
I am indwelling
And therefore will never leave you.

You are My child
And I love you.

Mine

Give it to me
And there it will remain.

It is mine now.

Let it remain with me.
Know that all is well
And working for your good.

God's Work

God's working with these hands.
God's working through these hands.

You have brought me
From bar stools to church pews
And I will to praise Your name.
From mountains high to valleys low
I need to praise Your name.

For all your glory and blessings
All my working days
And through all of my sleep filled nights
You will hear me praise Your name.

Jesus, my sweet Jesus
I will forever praise Your name.

Untitled

I am the vessel

Sometimes I give it to you in bits.
Everyday allowing some new miracle to occur,
So that you can add to your list . . .
And therefore add to the words of before.

Something short . . . will be enlogated.

Something little
—- much.

Just have faith and believeth in Me.
As I believeth in you.

I will provide all that you need.

You are unknowing to my final plan.

Have faith and let me lead.

Praise Him

. . . I . . . I can't say we
Because some of us know how
to praise Him.
So I have to say I.

I don't know how to praise Her
to the fullest
so that she can get the maximum.

Use to think that saying
Hallelujah was enough
. . . For it's the highest praise.
But . . .
the praise also involves
tone and pitch.

Giving things back over to God
And praying/worrying about it still
is not really giving it to God.

Give it to Her
. . . and begin to praise

Hallelujah isn't enough.

You gotta say

HALLELUJAH!
HALLELUJAH!

Scream it from the most inner
To the most outer.

Scream . . .

HALLELUJAH!

Get excited about it.
Get animated.

HALLELUJAH!

Act like you know that you know that you know
That everything is all right.

Say thank you
Because it's already taken care of . . .
It's already done.

Lift Me Up

My walk with You
Has not (always) been easy.

I fumble and stumble and fall.

. . . Lift me up.

I fear and doubt what you have shown me
there—
. . . just beyond my reach.

Lift me up.

Long for passions; (that I shouldn't)
—that might turn my whole life around.

Lift me up.

I am human

Lift me . . .
I pain and suffer—
struggle and fight.

Lift me, lift me up . . .

Lift me up so that I may do
Your will.

Lift me up
. . . Let me not forget.

Lift me up
so that I may . . . lift her up
. . . Lift him up.

No longer can it be . . . all about me
. . . all about me . . .
. . . all about me.

Now it is . . . all about me
. . . all about you . . .

all about we

all about us

all about this.

Me Today

Today,
I love me.

The Journey Back

As we start our new journey forward,
we should not forget to look back . . .
Back upon the history that has already
been laid.
Back to the struggle..
Back to the failures and achievements.

Let us not forget those that have gone before us
and give them homage for their
strength and courage.

Let us look back to
Amistad
(where the struggle for freedom began).

Let us look back to the Black Civil Rights Movement.

Let us look back to Stonewall and
The Unity Fellowship Church Movement.

Let us look back to Deacon Lucky
Audrey Lorde
Barbara Jordan
Dr. Majorie Hill
Carol Martin
Let us look back to our grandmothers and their mothers.

Let us look back to my mother and yours.
To our aunts and sisters.

Let us thank them all
For their strong bodies and faith.
For their support . . .
even if it was/is unspoken.

I implore you to look back and remember
all those that can before.
Give life and speak their names
. . . names of all those that
helped pave the way for you to be here.

No task is too small to measure.

Remember and give thanks.

Ashe

About the Author

Red was a nickname given to me by my father because I either had red hair as a youngster or because of the red hue that laid on my skin. I really don't know, but it became a term of endearment to me.

I grew up on the Lower East Side off of Houston Street, in Manhattan, along with my sister and two brothers. It wasn't until much later in my life, that I discovered that I had a younger brother as well.

Early on I knew that I was different from the other girls on the block. I liked trucks instead of dolls and toy guns instead of jump ropes; girls instead of boys.

Writing was my only outlet. It gave me a way to explore and explain (if to no one but myself). It became my way of safely expressing myself and probably saved me lots of money in therapy sessions. With my amateur style, I continued to write through college and then started to read my work to a select few.

I tried to do the hang out scene. The house parties, bars, clubs and many girlfriends but to tell you the truth, I really wasn't any good at that. I was a loner by nature. I began searching for more meaning to my life. I then discovered church. Maybe I shouldn't say discovered, but rather, became reacquainted with church and closer to the God of my understanding. As I continued to write and read, both in and out of church, at least one person would reveal to me that they felt the same way and thanked me for having the courage to share. It was the deeply felt "thank you" that nudged me to put some of my writings together under one cover. No one should feel that they are alone in their struggle to find themselves or without kindred spirits when standing in the truth that they find.

From the point that I began to recognize and listen to the voice of the God of my understanding, following the path She has laid and sharing with others the words placed upon my soul, my life took flight and blessings have been flowing ever since.

Whoever said that God doesn't bless the homosexual . . . lied.

God is in the blessing business. We just have to recognize HIS/HER voice and follow the path.

This book is a small collection of entries that have helped me through and I hope will help you through . . . whatever it is; just know that you are not alone.